Establishing Payment Arrangements: Beyond Net 30

Part of the Collecting Money Series
By Michelle Dunn

The economy continues to change causing more and more businesses to accept payments towards balances that are due if they want to get paid anything at all. Learn how to schedule payment plans that work for you and your customer. Learn the most efficient and effective ways to get your money in the quickest way possible. Learn how to predict which customers need payment plans before it is too late.

This book is designed to provide accurate information in regard to the subject matter covered. It is sold with the understanding that the author is not engaged in rendering legal advice or services.

ISBN #: 9781475187045

www.MichelleDunn.com   www.Credit-and-Collections.com

Table of Contents

Introduction

This book is for collectors and business owners who have customers that cannot pay in full like they may have in the past. Getting paid in full and receiving payments on account are two different things that have to be handled differently to be effective.

While the economy takes a nose dive business owners everywhere suddenly have to deal with setting up payment arrangements to help them get paid. Foreclosures are at a record high, people are losing their jobs in many industries making it more difficult to collect money. Credit flow through companies is drying up or non-existent at a rate not seen in decades.

When a customer cannot pay in full, payment arrangements must be made. The payment amount must be reasonable in comparison to the debt. When you set up the arrangements you must confirm the arrangements in writing and record them in your computer on the customers' account. Failure to take these steps will result in your payment arrangement failing.

What are your terms?

As a business owner, when you make a sale, do you know when you will be paid? Controlling when you get paid is a huge component on whether your business will survive or fail. If you extend credit to any customers, new or existing, outline how and when you want to be paid. Be specific on each factor and let customers know what will happen if they do not meet those payment requirements. Something to remember is that if you don't set the payment terms for your business, your customers will. The terms you set are to protect your rights, limit your liabilities, and provide you with some security that you will get paid.

When are your bills due?

Make sure when you set up your payment terms you get paid in time to pay your bills. You may also be interested in taking advantage of pre-pay or early pay discounts. This can save you hundreds of dollars over the course of a year.

Your terms should outline how and when you want to be paid as well as the circumstances that will follow if the payments are not made as agreed. Once a week, or at least twice a month, print out and take a good look at your accounts receivables aging report, are customers becoming slower in their payments as the economy continues to falter? Follow up with those customers now and get them back on track, maybe with a payment plan if they cannot pay in full at this time.

Some things you can do to improve your cash flow and help your customers pay your invoices:

- Offer discounts.
- Get 50% down at the time of the order
- Check each customer's credit.

- Sell old outdated inventory on sale.
- Issue invoices immediately.
- Follow up right away with slow paying customers.
- Offer payment arrangements.
- Use a different color paper to print your invoice and statements.
- Use a larger font on the total amount due and underline it twice.
- Have a call to action on your invoices in a large font, in a bright color, something such as PAY NOW or PAY IMMEDIATELY in red, blue or green ink.
- Include postage paid or pre-addressed payment envelopes and include them with the invoice and/or statements.
- Stamp or print an important message on the outside of the envelope you mail your bills in, you can use a rubber stamp or your printer, some examples:
  - Dated material
  - As Requested
  - Confidential
  - Do Not Bend
  - Handle with Care
  - Personal

Some things to think about when you are setting your payment terms:

- How often do you want to get paid?
- Do you want to get paid at the time of sale or service or do you want to offer something like 30 day terms?
- Maybe you want to offer 30 day terms with a discount if the invoice is paid in full within 10 or 15 days.

When will receiving this money benefit you most? Maybe right before your bills are due so you have the money on hand to pay your bills on time or take advantage of early pay discounts and saving even more money. When setting your terms, choose a time of the month that you want to be paid, such as the first of the month or the 15th, any date that works best for your business.

Make sure your invoices and statements include the following:

- Your address, URL, email address, and toll free number if you have one.
- Your price, any discounts, and a final and total price.
- Delivery specifications or directions; always include a phone number.
- Your payment terms.
- Your discount program in detail.
- Any late fee or interest program in detail.
- Notice that you will seek compensation for any debt-recovery costs if not paid according to your terms and conditions.

Here is an example of how your payment terms may be set up, but this would be customized for your particular business:

Example of Payment Terms

A. Payment terms are net thirty (30) days from the date of invoice. Seller reserves the right to require alternative payment terms, including, without limitation, a letter of credit or payment in advance.

B. If payment is not received by the due date, a late charge will be added at the rate of one and one-half percent (1.5%) per month eighteen percent (18%) per year or the maximum legal rate, whichever is less, to unpaid invoices from the due date thereof.

C. All payments by check should be sent to:
   Your address
   All payments by wire transfer should be submitted to:
   Your bank name, address and contact person.

D. If buyer is delinquent in paying any amount owed to seller by more than ten (10) days, then without limiting any other rights and remedies available to seller under the law, in equity, or under contract, seller may suspend production, shipment, and/or deliveries of any or all products purchased by buyer, or by notice to buyer, treat such delinquency as a repudiation by buyer of the portion of the contract not then fully performed, whereupon the seller may cancel all further deliveries and any amounts unpaid hereunder shall immediately become due and payable. If the seller has to retain a collection agency or lawyer to collect overdue amount, all collection costs, including attorney fees and court costs shall be payable by the buyer.

E. Have a line under these statements on everything you print them on and have the customer sign and date it, keep the original and give the customer a copy.

Objectives of payment arrangements

The reason you offer payment arrangements on a balance due is so you can improve your cash flow while helping your customers. You want to effectively outline policies and procedures that will help provide your customers with options when they cannot pay in full. If you don't there won't be any guidelines and when you are accepting payments on account you want all your ducks in a row.

The more options for payment for any of the services or products you offer, the better your chances of making a sale and getting paid promptly. If you only do business on a cash basis, you miss out on a lot of good sales opportunities. There are many different options available for you to use. Some common forms of payment can be:

- Credit Cards
- Debit Cards
- Personal and business checks
- Wire transfer
- Online payments
- Money orders
- Cash

Right now, with the economy a mess and more and more consumers unable to pay their bills, the objective of your payment arrangements is to at least be getting paid something rather than nothing. Offering payments arrangements can save your business from going out of business by offering realistic plans for people who can't pay in full but can pay something. Your objective is to get paid *SOMETHING*.

Most customers will look at all their bills and then make a decision on which ones will get paid that month based on what is most important to them. It is your job to make your invoice important to them and to offer them realistic options so that they will pay it each month. Mortgage payments normally come first on that list, followed by things like food, phone, electricity, fuel and daycare.

How payment arrangements affect your business

Something to remember if you don't like the idea of offering payment plans. If someone owes you money, they probably owe others money and whoever takes action first or offers a solution, will get paid first.

There has never been a more important time for you to offer payment arrangements to your customers. When you are able to work with your customers to set up realistic payment plans and goals you will:

- Increase profits and revenues
- Retain customers
- Improve your operational efficiency
- Increase your bottom line
- Minimize your risk
- Have less bad debt
- Be able to efficiently handle and control your accounts receivables

Identifying which accounts need payment arrangements and contacting those customers before they become overdue will dramatically affect the bottom line of your business. Identifying and working with these customers will maximize your cash flow.

REMEMBER: *You do not have to accept a check as a form of payment if you think it presents a risk. Acceptance of a check as a form of payment is a privilege extended by you. Cash and checks are NOT the same thing. When you accept a check you are crediting a customer with having sufficient funds in the bank to cover the check.*

Payment arrangements will affect your business by providing you with some cash flow where you may not have had any. By offering payment arrangements when the economy and country is in a crisis, you extend a helping hand to your customers and your community while enabling your business to continue to stay in business and become more successful. If you do not offer payment arrangements in these tough economic times you may have much lower cash flow, you may lose customers and you may become unable to pay your own bills resulting in your business going out of business or filing for bankruptcy.

Offering payment plans let your customer budget a set amount each month to pay to you, this can help them when money is tight because they know the exact amount they need to pay each month which is easier for them to handle than maybe making the entire payment. Thus you will get paid, but over time instead of a lump sum. This can also benefit your business because instead of not getting any of the money, you get a bit each month and can use that towards paying your own business bills.

Elements that affect payment arrangements

Business owners everywhere are struggling to stay in business; many are filing bankruptcy or simply closing their doors. Some aspects of business that may not have been getting the attention needed due to the booming economy are now under scrutiny. If your business is struggling due to the economy change is imperative to your success. Offering payment arrangements is more important now than ever before.

Business owners and consumers are encountering problems they have not had to deal with before and don't know how to handle them. For example, many are finding that customers who have always been able to pay on time are having trouble paying their bills and staying current. Other customers who may have been slow payers are falling even further behind or are unable to pay at all.

You need to create positive steps you can utilize to keep your existing customers, get paid and stay in business. Some tools that you need to do this include offering payment arrangements, procedures and actions that are clearly outlined so that when someone cannot pay or has a problem paying you know what to do immediately and can take steps to help that customer and help yourself.

As more and more people across the U.S. lose their jobs and become victims of the recession, your job becomes tougher trying to collect from your customers who may have a drastically less income or in some cases, no income at all. How can you collect from someone who can barely pay their living expenses?

If someone is not working they might have other sources of income to pay off debts. They may have credit cards they can use to tide them over until they get a job. During this credit crisis, the advice for working folks is to STOP using their credit cards but if your customer is not working but maybe collecting unemployment, this may be an avenue that is open to them when they don't have many other options. Once they do get a job and have a regular income they can stop using their credit cards and pay them off as quickly as possible. You can also suggest they visit a reputable credit counseling service in their area for help.

When to set up payment arrangements

Print out a current accounts receivable listing and look at your customers' accounts, what they owe, how much they owe, how old it is, their payment history and when was the last time their credit limit was reviewed? Once you see this information, you will notice which customers might need to set up a payment arrangement.

Some things to look for are larger balances due than in the past, they are taking longer to pay now than they have been in the past, they have stopped ordering from you and paying you. If you notice any of these things, now is the time to set up payment arrangements with those customers and customers who might be past due in general or are due now but you haven't received a check.

You should think about setting up payment arrangements when you find yourself unable to pay your own bills on time, or you find your daily deposits are much smaller than they have been or when you find that your customers are not paying like they have in the past. It is important to stay on top of these things and start offering payment plans before any of these things becomes a bigger problem. Nipping cash flow issues in the bud is a very important part of payment plans.

How to set up payment arrangements

You only need to set up payment arrangements if a customer cannot make payment in full. You must always make the arrangement by talking with the customer, and then you MUST follow up by sending a written notice or letter reiterating what that arrangement is. The only way to make this work is to be very specific. The first line of your letter should say something like, "As per our conversation today and put the date of the call" then go on to state the terms you agreed to, the total due, the number of payments, the due date of each payment and the amount of each payment, I cannot stress enough that you need to be very specific. Also, include a payment envelope if you can, because the easier you make it for the customer to pay, the better your chances are of getting paid.

Never start a call with a customer by asking them how much they can pay; this is just setting yourself up for failure. To be in control of the call you must let the customer know how much you can accept not the other way around. Once you ask the debtor how much they can pay, you lose all negotiations and you lose control of the call and the situation.

Some of you are new to setting up payment arrangements or might even be new to calling the customers. It is essential to communicate confidence when you are speaking to past due customers. You must be relaxed, confident, and prepared. Remember, everything you do represents your company: How you speak, how you collect money, send out invoices, and handle tough situations. Some things to consider when speaking to customers and making payments arrangements:

First impressions – When your customer realizes you are calling about a past due invoice, they will not be happy. You must portray confidence, smile when you speak into the phone, it will be noticeable in your voice.

Your voice should be loud enough to be heard and sound confident, not to loud but not to soft. You want your customer to hear you and understand everything you are saying. Sit up straight in your chair and imagine this person is sitting across from you.

Maintain "eye contact" by staying focused on the call. Don't check your email or watch the other people in your office. Stay focused.

Relax! Sit up straight in your chair; don't play with paperclips or pens on your desk. Use your face, voice, and posture to send your confidence over the phone and in person.

If you put these techniques into effect, you will collect more money and have better results from the calls you make. Take steps to ensure you make your calls in the most effective way the first time, so you don't have to continue to make calls to people that you let have control of the situation.

When deciding how to set up each customer on their specific payment plan, decide how many monthly payments you can extend to the customer, then divide the total amount due by the number of months you want the balance to be paid in. This will be the monthly payment.

Make sure when you set up a payment arrangement with any customer that you PUT IT IN WRITING. This is very important. Let the customer know that if they cannot make a payment, to call you and let you know, don't just skip the payment because this could void the payment agreement. This way you will keep the lines of communication open with your customer, while helping them to stay on track and keeping some cash flow through your business.

Why offer payment arrangements

The most important reason you want to offer payment arrangements is to get paid. In this troubled economy it is unrealistic to think your customers can all pay you in full, if a customer is avoiding you or becoming more and more delinquent, it is likely they just cannot pay the entire bill and don't realize they have the opportunity to set up a payment plan. In my years of doing collection work, many of the debtors I would call did not pay because they thought they had to pay the whole amount, Once they realized they could set up a payment plan, they were relieved and open to setting something up to get their bill paid. The key in offering payment arrangements, especially now, is to BE REALISTIC.

If you treat your customers well, they will continue to be your customer when this economic crisis is over, they will appreciate that you worked with them and hopefully continue to be loyal and tell others about your business.

Assessing the situation

Many business owners don't set precedence on payment plans, they accept whatever their customer offers without any negotiation, this is a huge mistake that can cost you the customer, money or your business. Business owners need to maximize their in-house receivables, they cannot get a handle on their receivables without assessing the situation and negotiating a payment plan that works for them, the customer and that is beneficial to all involved.

You have to make payment arrangements that are worth your while, while making the arrangement do-able for the customer. If you set up a blanket payment arrangement, for example, everyone pays $100 a month, if a debtor cannot pay that, you will not get paid. If you work with the debtor and assess their specific situation and agree on $25 every other week, and the customer can do that, you will get paid.

Some tips to help you deal with customers who may need payment plans:

- Keep an eye on your accounts receivables and credit limits.
- Send your bill upon completion of the work, don't wait 30 days.
- Offer more payment options.
- Make collection calls and set up any payment plans with someone with authority, not an assistant or clerk.
- Be persistent and follow up.
- Hold orders until balances have been paid.
- Communicate!

If a customer suddenly comes into a lump sum of money you may want to offer a settlement amount rather than payment arrangements. This way the customer pays off the debt for a lesser amount but in one lump sum, so you get a bigger payment all at once. You will have to decide if you can afford to write off any portion of the debt, such as late fees, interest or shipping charges or anything else, then offer the customer a lump sum settlement payment and give it a due date. If they can't pay the settlement amount in one lump sum by the specified date, the offer is void. I have done this with great success, something to look for is when people get their tax returns, Christmas club checks, or a severance package from work. If they can't afford a settlement payment, go back to setting up a payment plan, but explain to them that the payment plan is on the entire balance due, they only get the lesser balance due if they can make the settlement payment in full by a certain date. As with any payment plan or settlement offer, put it in writing.

Specific steps for successful payment arrangements

1. Ask for payment in full.
2. If the customer cannot pay in full, offer to split the balance due into two payments.
3. If that is not possible, it is time to negotiate by gathering more information on the customers' financial status.
4. Ask open ended questions so you can evaluate the situation.
5. Suggest weekly or bi-monthly payments, as opposed to the common monthly payments.
6. Come to an agreement that is beneficial to you and the customer.
7. Get a commitment and document it.
8. Send the customer a letter reiterating your understanding of the agreement.
9. Ask for a signature on the agreement.

Always start off asking for the payment in full, then go down from there. Always aim high, such as first asking for 100% then 80% then 75% etc. If you leave it up to the customer they will offer the lowest possible amount and that may not help you in your situation at all and certainly won't help them. Based on the economy and how it stands now, you may have to get some pretty small payments but try to get as much as you can as frequently as you can.

- Send a confirmation letter the day you make the payment arrangement with the customer.
- Send a payment reminder 10 days before the payment is due.
- On the due date if you do not have payment, send a letter giving them 5 days to pay before the arrangement is revoked and they go back to full collections on the full amount.

Another example might be that once you have the owner of the business or the debtor on the phone, identify yourself and your company and state the purpose of your call. If the person tells you they cannot pay anything, listen to them and ask specific questions to help you offer a solution to the debtor.

You might ask things such as:

- Do you have a job?
- Does your spouse have a job?
- Are you collecting unemployment?
- When do you get paid?

Learn as much as you can about their financial situation and their other bills so you can help to offer a realistic payment plan. If your payment plan is not realistic, it will not happen.

Send a confirmation letter that day, confirming your conversation and the date as well as all payment details. Include how much will be paid on which date and in how many payments, you might want to include what will happen if the arrangements are not met. Offer to re-evaluate their payment arrangement if their financial situation changes.

Skills & resources for setting up payment plans

Anyone who is trying to collect money, even if the amount was agreed upon at the time of the sale, needs to know how to negotiate. Some skills you will need in order to be a good negotiator:

Understanding the negotiation process – highly effective collectors recognize that negotiations are a process. It requires an understanding of the billing, credit approval and payment processes.

Focusing on a Win-Win situation – Win-win means that both parties feel like they have "won" during the collection process. Great bill collectors' help their customers try to solve problems and look for opportunities to make that possible. They also know when to be firm and limit what they do in order to reach an agreement that is acceptable for both parties.

Patience – Too many collectors try to go for the "quick fix" so they can get paid and move on to the next account. Good bill collectors know that patience is a virtue and that rushing the collection process only leads to not getting paid. Gather information BEFORE contacting your customer, then think carefully about possible solutions and this is really critical because major mistakes can be made when you rush.

Confidence – Good collectors are confident when making a call or writing a letter. They aren't arrogant, rude or cocky, they are confident and helpful. You must believe in your ability to reach a win-win agreement with the customer, this is obtained through experience.

Listening skills – People will tell you just about everything you need to know if you ask the right questions or keep quiet long enough for them to continue speaking. The biggest mistake a bill collector can make is not listening or bigger yet, interrupting a customer when that might mean if they had just listened longer, they may have received key information that would assist them in their collection effort. When you call a customer and you state the reason for your call or ask a question, wait for the answer. No matter how long the pause may be, let the customer break that silence with an answer.

Some other skills needed to be able to work with your customers to get paid, or set up payment arrangements are:

Managing the emotional side – customers will get upset that you are calling them. They have bigger and better things to think about other than your bill, they will cry, yell at you, hang up on you and swear at you. When a customer starts to tell you their life history and how this affects how they pay you, you need to be able to have some compassion but offer a solution to get the bill paid. This is when you would offer a payment plan or different payment options.

Prepare a pre-call plan: before you ever call a customer about their balance, you need to research their account. Before you dial, make sure you know the invoice number, date, amount that is past due, how past due it is, the payment history, details of the order and if there were any disputed items. When the customer asks you any question, you need to answer immediately whenever possible, otherwise you lose time and time is money.

Having an opening statement ready – your opening statement should be very brief and to the point. You need to identify yourself and your company, state why you are calling and what you want.

For example:

"Hi, this is Michelle from KTM Auto calling about your past due balance of $500.00 on invoice #1234 dated 4/1/08. I am calling today to take your payment over the phone to clear this balance from your account. Would you like to pay with a credit or debit card or check by phone?"

STOP

WAIT for an answer and always assume the debtor will pay. This is the point where they may tell you they can't pay in full and you would proceed to start setting up a payment plan.

Ask questions – asking questions with precision and making the transition to the payment arrangement – all your questions should be clear and to the point with silence after each question, so the customer can answer. Make sure you LISTEN.

For example:

Customer: I can't pay, I don't have any money.
You: Are you working?
Customer: Yes, but I just started a job and don't get paid for 2 weeks.
You: What day will you get paid?
Customer: Friday
You: Okay, we can accept a payment of half the balance on Saturday.

This can go on and on, the customer might then tell you they can't pay half, you work down from there until you reach a realistic agreement. Then send out a confirmation letter with all the details of the agreement. Then you call on Friday to remind them about making that payment.

For example:

"Hi this is Michelle from KTM Auto calling to confirm you will be mailing your check for $50 tomorrow, Saturday as we agreed."

Anyone working with your customers to set up payment arrangements needs to:

- Be interest in people, and be a good communicator both verbally and in writing.
- Be persuasive and persistent, with the sensitivity to deal fairly with people in often difficult situations.
- Be able to stay calm under pressure, and be adaptable in sometimes tricky situations.
- Have strong negotiation skills and the ability to explain financial matters firmly and clearly.
- Have mathematical ability to explain payments, financial terms and credit services and policies.
- Be able to understand relevant legislation concerning data protection and harassment.
- Have office administration and computer skills.

Elements of a payment plan

1. Contact is made with the customer.
2. You ask for payment in full, the customer lets you know that is not possible and asks for a payment plan.
3. You ask the debtor basic questions regarding their finances
    a. Are you working?
    b. Is your spouse/significant other/roommate working?
    c. When do you get paid?
    d. What other debts do you have to pay? (Credit cards, car payments, day care etc.)
    e. Are you receiving unemployment?
    f. How are you paying your bills now?
    g. What is your profession or what do you do?
    h. How much do you make an hour or week?
4. Ask questions that will help you to determine the approximate disposable income of the customer.
5. Depending on the amount of income the customer has and the amount owed, make a realistic estimate on what you would like to ask for in terms of monthly, weekly, bi-weekly etc, payments.
6. Offer more than one option to the customer so they have a part in the decision and are more likely to make those payments.

Why should you offer payment plans?

When you are setting up payment arrangements it is a two way street, you create the rules and your customers have to play by them if they want to do business with you. It is up to you to be fair, reasonable and not to be intimidating.

You want to offer payment plans to keep cash flowing through your business, if you have customers that can't realistically pay in full, and you don't offer them a payment arrangement, you won't get any money. If you offer payment options, you will get your money but over time. Getting paid something each month is better than not getting paid anything at all.

Tracking payment plans

Once you make a payment plan agreement with the customer, you need to track it. Make sure when you set up the payment plan you let the customer know that if they miss one payment they will then be asked to pay in full, if that is your intention. You may want to send letters with payment envelopes a few days before each payment is due, and if a payment is missed, follow up immediately if not sooner! Always make an effort to get a customer back on track before taking further action.

Utilize statements, most software offers printing statements as an option. Send out monthly statements to all your customers but specifically those with payment arrangements. This will show them their balance due, what payments were made and the dates and how much is still due.

Missed payments and how to correct them

When a customer that has been set up on a payment plan misses a payment, call them immediately. Let them know you need the payment right then over the phone or the account will go back to the collection department, and further action may be taken. Further action could be, reporting to the credit bureau, putting their account on hold, revoking their credit all together, placing them with an outside collection agency or maybe small claims court. Remember that whatever you tell the customer you "might" do, if they do not follow through with the payment, you must take those action. Never threaten something you don't intend to follow through on. You will lose all credibility and all chances of getting paid.

When you set up the initial payment arrangement, you would have sent them something in writing, hopefully your document also let them know that if they missed a payment or a payment was late that the payment arrangement would become null and void and the total balance would now be due. Most times that is enough to keep someone on track, especially if they know they cannot come up with the full balance to pay in full. Keeping on top of customers that you set up on payment arrangements is very important, you must become their babysitter and keep them on track.

Top methods for improving payment plans

Letting the customer know you care about their account and their situation enough to work with them to help them to get their bill paid is one of the top methods to improve your payment plans and collections. Another top method for improving your payment plan is to offer the customer something that they perceive as "special treatment" for example, can you write off some interest, or late fees, or lower their interest rate for 3 or 6 months? This gives them some confidence that as they pay their balance is actually going down, and not going up with interest. Another method might be offering to void the final payment if all other payment are made on time. Offering incentives has a huge impact on how you are paid. You may be able to offer something such as suspending all collection calls or activity on the account during the time of the payment plan. Offer many different ways to pay, money orders, western union, checks, credit card, debit card, online payment options, or in person. You can also get the checks up front; say you set up a customer for make 6 monthly payments of $25.00. Have them send you the 6 checks, each one dated for the month it is due.

   a. Work with the customer.
   b. Offer "special treatment".
   c. Offer incentives.
   d. Suspend collection activity as they make payments.
   e. Offer many payment options.
   f. Get checks up front.

Following up

If you do everything you just learned about setting up payment arrangements and then skip this step, you may not get paid. Following up with the customers that you give special payment arrangements to is critical to your success and to your getting paid. Many customers will be very agreeable on the phone when you are setting up a payment plan, but once they hang up they forget all about it. This is why it is imperative that you send the agreement in writing immediately after speaking to them, and monitor their account to make sure they are making the payments as agreed.

It is a lot like babysitting, but if you don't do it, you may not get paid at all. Stay on top of your payment plan accounts by printing out aging reports weekly or setting up a tickler file so you know when to contact a customer that is not making their payments as agreed. If you told your customers that if they missed a payment the agreement would be null and void, follow through with that or you will never have any credibility or leverage with that customer again.

Sometimes offering an incentive such as if you make all of the payments on time or early, we will waive the last payment, will keep customers on track.

Another good follow up tool is to send a letter or notice each time you receive a payment, that start out with "Thank you for your payment of $25.00, your new balance is $150.00 and your next payment is due Friday, march 20, 2009. I have enclosed a payment envelope for your next payment."

Stay on top of it and you increase your chances for success. This may seem like a lot of work on your part, but if you don't put the effort in, you will not get paid.

RESOURCES

My blog www.Credit-and-Collections.com

A Business Guide to Getting customers to Pay networking group
http://www.linkedin.com/groups/Business-Guide-getting-
customers-pay-2652085?

Videos about setting up payment plans
http://www.youtube.com/user/MichelleDunn1/videos

The following is an excerpt from Getting Paid using Social Media

Social Media Success Tips

For many collectors the first thing they do to try to locate a debtor or get information is visit social networks. People make themselves very easy to be found and post all kinds of personal information that makes your job easier. Some of the top things you can find posted on social networks are:

- Birth date
- Address
- Employment information
- Asset information

With a name and a birth date a collector can search public records on an individual.

Top 4 tips of what you can do to have more success using social networks to locate debtors, and better your business:

1. Everyone is doing it, this is one time when you should follow the pack and participate
2. Listen, just like any networking event listen before you "talk"
3. Track conversations with keywords, names, company names, executives names and use Google Reader and Google Blog Search (both free) to track them.
4. Practice participating in social medias so you understand how they work. Many people, who might be a debtor, spend hours on these websites and know them inside and out.

Common mistakes

When you use a social networking site to locate a debtor, to then try to collect from them by phone, or mail, there normally won't be a problem. The problems arise when someone contacts a debtor through one of these social websites. Since the information, messages or conversations on these types of websites is not private and is available to many people to see, this would not be a tool to use in debt collection without violating federal laws specifically applicable to consumer debt collections. Most of these types of websites are integrated with electronic mail and one can send email to one specific person, BUT, just how private is this? How can you be sure? Better safe than sorry – don't utilize the email tools on these websites to contact someone who owes money. You can run into legal problems and violate privacy laws.

Use private or provided email addresses when contacting your customers that want to be contacted by email and keep a record of every correspondence.

Top 10 Social Media Collections Tips

1. Use private or provided email addresses when contacting your customers that want to be contacted by email and keep a record of every correspondence.

2. Never converse with a debtor using social media sites, utilizing the email feature or comment feature.

3. Do not email a debtor about a debt if you think a third party can ever see that email.

4. Do not instant message a debtor about a debt.

5. If a debtor doesn't respond to your email after authorizing you to email them, stop emailing and use traditional methods to try and collect, such as phone calls or letters.

6. Do not send any communication that could be seen by a third party.

7. Never "publish" a list of names of debtors anywhere online.

8. Do not make false reports to a credit bureau.

9. Do not use a fake name or company name.

10. Do not request to be added as a "friend" by a debtor on a social networking site

5 clues that your customer is not going to pay you

There isn't a business out there that is immune to slow payers or non-paying customers, but what can you do to prevent this from happening? Keeping an eye on your customers' accounts is an important part of preventing bad debt or payment problems. I would like to share some "red flags" with you that can help you identify when a customer is having financial problems or is just not going to pay you or pay you on time:

1. No communication – once the communication between your company and your customer is broken down that is a red flag that your customer can't or won't pay. Keep the lines of communication open at all times in order to avoid this.

2. Waiting until an account is already past terms to bring up disputes such as pricing problems, shortages, or billing issues. It is up to you to "babysit" your customers' accounts to make sure they stay on track – contact customers before the invoice is due to resolve any issues so the bill can still be paid on time.

3. Broken payment promises with no real reason other than I forgot, was on vacation or I thought I mailed that! Keep an eye on this type of account – and check out the customers' social media pages – if they can go on vacation – they can pay your bill or at the very least set up a payment plan.

4. They paid for their last order that was on payment hold with a bad check in order to get another order shipped. Any account that gives you a bad check needs to be re-evaluated. Re-check credit, get cash for the bad check and any fees and

revoke their credit, make sure to get pre-payment or COD, cash only for any future orders.

5. The mail is returned and the phone is disconnected. Check the original credit application and/or contract for additional contact information; check their social networking pages for new cell phone numbers or addresses. If you are unable to re-establish contact, place them with a collection agency or take them to small claims court yourself if the amount due allows.

3 things you must do immediately when a customer is overdue

It happens to all of us. We know our customers, and they would never stiff us. Until....it happens to you. A customer that has always paid on time is paying slower than in the past and is becoming increasingly past due.

Most business owners don't even realize a customer is getting more and more behind until they owe a large sum of money and it is over 60 days past due. What do you do now?

If you don't have any procedures in place for this type of situation there are 3 things you must do right now in order to get this customer back on track and get your cash flowing again.

1. Call them! Make sure everything is ok, ask what you can do to help them pay your bills on time and get a payment promise today.
2. Send a letter following up on your call – mail it today! It can be short and sweet but must be very specific. Make sure to mention how much will be paid and by what date.
3. FOLLOW UP! If you get a machine, call again tomorrow AND send a letter.

These seem like simple things that won't make a difference but they will make a huge difference. Try it on 5-10 accounts this week and you will notice more payments coming in. Once you start getting return calls and more checks in the mail it will motivate you to do this for all of your past due customers!

Getting Paid in a Bad Economy

Business owners everywhere are asking me how they can get paid when their customers are suffering with job loss, house loss and the rising prices of everything in this tough economy. Should they be more lenient or maybe tougher when accounts become late or past due?

Something to consider when you are thinking about being lenient with customers that are past due is that if someone owes you money, they probably owe others money and whoever takes action first, will get paid first.

Here are a few tips that will help you get paid while the economy is suffering:

1. Get paid at the time of service or if you offer terms invoice customers on a regular basis and as soon as the work is complete, and make sure your invoices have the due date clearly visible.
2. Change your payment terms, if your terms are net 60 or net 45 change them to net 30 or net 15, you can also offer an early payment discount to anyone who pays early, such as 1 or 2% off the bill if they pay within 10 days.
3. Act early - call big accounts or accounts with large balances 10 days BEFORE the invoice is due to make sure they have the invoice, that they have the correct address to send the check and that there are no problems and that the bill is scheduled to be paid.
4. When setting up payment plans remember that you want as much as you can get as frequently as you can get it.
5. If a business owes you money, visit them. If it is a restaurant, go there for lunch, if it is a printing company, get something printed or copied. Every time you walk in

they will see you and it reminds them that they owe you money.
6. Use a collection agency.

Collecting money is like cleaning the bathroom, no one likes to do it but it must get done. If you don't want to do it, hire someone to do it for you. Getting paid keeps cash flowing, so it is imperative to make sure you are getting paid, and getting paid according to the terms you set for your business.

Taking any or all of these steps will only help you to collect money in the short term but without making changes, such as having a credit policy, or checking credit BEFORE extending credit, you will be right back where you started next month.

BONUS: Letter example

Partial Payment Letter

Debtor name
Debtor address
Debtor city, state, zip

Date

RE: Account balance

Account number

Dear Debtor:

Thank you for your payment of $_____ towards your balance.
The balance due of $_____ remains past due.

Please mail your check for $_____ today.

A postpaid envelope is enclosed for your payment.

Sincerely,

Thank you for buying my book, I hope it was helpful to you. If you liked it, please leave a review on Amazon. Thank you!

Other books by Michelle

Please look for other books by Michelle Dunn on Amazon.com and MichelleDunn.com – most titles are now available for Kindle.

Join me on LinkedIn and Twitter @DunnMich

About the author

In 1998, when Michelle was getting a divorce and had 2 small children, she started a collection agency from home leaving her full time job 6 months later. Her agency did very well and grew over the next 8 years until Michelle sold it to write full time.

Michelle knew what business owners needed and had already written a couple of books that were selling well. "But it was still a huge leap", she says, "I was a single mom with two sons." I started putting together my ideas, set up a office in my home, and used the income from book sales to fund publishing more books.

That same year Michelle self published 4 books and e-books before landing her first book contract with Entrepreneur Press to write The Ultimate Credit and Collections Handbook, the check IS in the mail. She then self published a couple more business books before getting a book deal with John Wiley & Sons Publishing for her first hardcover book, The Guide to Getting Paid, weed out bad paying customers, collect on past due balances, and avoid bad debt.

To learn more, visit www.MichelleDunn.com and www.Credit-and-Collections.com